Mel Bay's First Lessons

Rock Guitar Method

by Corey Christiansen
and Mike Christiansen

2 3 4 5 6 7 8 9 0

CD CONTENTS

1	Tuning
2	Exercise 1
3	Exercise 2
4	Exercise 3
5	Exercise 4
6	Strum Patterns
7	Strum Pattern 1
8	Strum Pattern 2
9	Strum Pattern 3
10	Any Time
11	Choices
12	Think It Over
13	Under The Arch
14	So Smooth
15	Waiting For You
16	Loss For Words
17	Freezing Point
18	Send Help
19	Fourth Gear
20	Fifth Gear
21	Overdrive
22	E Shuffle
23	Power Chords 1
24	Power Chords 2
25	The Watchtower
26	Flying High
27	Summer Blues, Summer Not
28	Licks 1 & 2
29	Lick 3
30	Lick 4
31	Lick 5
32	You Know What I Mean
33	Moveable Power Chords 1
34	Moveable Power Chords 2
35	Moveable Power Chords 3
36	Moveable Power Chords 4
37	Moveable Power Chords 5

It doesn't get any easier.....

Visit us on the Web at www.melbay.com — E-mail us at email@melbay.com

Introduction

This beginning guitar method is unique because the style of music used throughout the entire book is rock. Using the rock music as the vehicle, this method presents the fundamentals of playing guitar. Accompaniment and solo techniques are presented. The book contains sections on strumming, reading standard notation and tablature, power chords, and the scales used in building an improvised solo.

This book is written so it can be studied front to back, or by skipping from section to section. For example, one could learn the basic chords and strum patterns, then skip to the section which presents notes on the first two strings. After learning those notes, one could skip to the section on power chords.

Parts of the Guitar

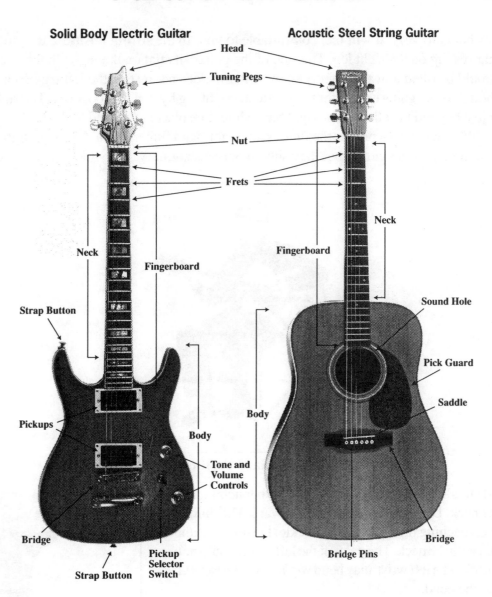

Solid Body Electric Guitar   Acoustic Steel String Guitar

Head
Tuning Pegs
Nut
Frets
Neck
Fingerboard
Strap Button
Pickups
Body
Bridge
Strap Button
Tone and Volume Controls
Pickup Selector Switch
Fingerboard
Sound Hole
Pick Guard
Saddle
Body
Bridge
Bridge Pins

Care of the Guitar

Here are some tips to keep in mind for taking care of the guitar:

1) Make sure the correct type of strings are on the guitar. There are basically two types of strings: nylon and steel. Nylon strings are used on the classical guitar and steel strings are used on the steel string acoustic (folk) guitar and electric guitar (unless the electric has an "acoustic" pick-up). Steel strings which are bronze are for the steel string acoustic guitar. Bronze strings do not work well on electric guitars unless the electric has an "acoustic pick-up". Most guitars play best if they are strung with medium or light gauge strings. Note: heavy gauge strings may warp the neck on some guitars.

2) Avoid rapid temperature and/or humidity changes. A rapid change could damage the finish and the wood of the guitar. Do not leave the guitar in a car when the weather is very hot or cold, and try not to leave the guitar next to heater vents or air conditioners. If the climate is extremely dry, a guitar humidifier can be used to prevent the guitar from drying and cracking.

3) Polish the guitar. Polish which is made specifically for guitars can be purchased from a music store. Besides keeping the guitar looking nice, polishing the guitar will help protect the finish and the woods. Be careful not to polish the fingerboard.

4) If the guitar is being shipped or taken on an airplane, always loosen the strings. The strings do not have to be completely loose, but should be loose enough that the tension of the strings pulling on the neck is greatly reduced.

Holding Position

If the guitar is held properly, it will feel comfortable to you. In the **sitting position,** the guitar is held with the waist of the guitar resting on the right leg. The side of the guitar sits flat on the leg with the neck extending to the left. The neck should be tilted upward slightly so the left arm does not rest on the left leg. Both feet should be flat on the floor, although some guitarists prefer to elevate the right leg by using a footstool. The right arm rests on the top of the guitar just beyond the elbow. The right hand should be placed over and to the back (towards the bridge) of the sound hole. Whether using a pick or the fingers, the right-hand fingers should be bent slightly. The right-hand fingers may touch the top of the guitar, but they should not be stationary. They move when stroking the strings.

Standard Position

The left hand should be positioned with the thumb touching the back of the guitar neck. Do not bend the thumb forward. The thumb should be vertical, touching the neck at the knuckle. Do not position the thumb parallel with the neck. The palm of the left hand should not touch the guitar neck. The left wrist may bend *slightly,* but be careful not to exaggerate the bend.

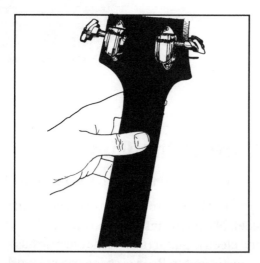

When placing a left-hand finger on the string, "square" the finger and push on the string using the tip of the finger. (The fingernails must be short so the tip of the finger can be used.) The finger should be positioned just behind and touching (when possible) the fret wire. Placing the finger too low in the fret may result in a buzz, and placing the finger on top of the fret wire may cause a muted sound. The left-hand knuckles should run parallel with the guitar neck. This makes it possible to reach higher frets with the left-hand third and fourth fingers without turning the wrist. Again, be careful not to bring the left-hand thumb over the top of the guitar neck, and do not touch the guitar neck with the palm of the hand, When pushing on the string, it is as though the guitar neck and string are being pinched between the thumb and finger.

Push the string firmly enough to get a sound, but don't over push. To determine the correct amount of pressure, touch the string with the left-hand finger and gradually apply pressure. Pick the string over and over. When a clear sound occurs, that's the amount of pressure to use.

4

Rest your right-hand thumb on the first (the smallest) string and stroke the open string (open means no left-hand fingers are pushing on the string) downward. Make sure the right-hand wrist moves, and the arm moves slightly from the elbow. The right-hand fingers may touch the top of the guitar, but they should move when the string is played. Try to have a relaxed feeling in the right hand. Go straight down with the thumb when stroking the string. Next, with the right-hand thumb, play the second string open. When playing a string other than the first string, the thumb should go straight down and rest upon (but not play) the next smallest string. In classic guitar playing, this is called a **rest stroke.**

Strumming refers to playing three or more strings so the strings sound simultaneously. To practice the strumming action, rest the right-hand thumb on the fourth string and strum four strings. Using a down stroke, let the right hand fall quickly across the strings so they sound at the same time. The right-hand wrist and arm move with the action.

To hold the pick correctly, first, bend the right-hand index finger. The other fingers of the right hand also bend, but not as much as the index finger.

The pick is placed on the end of the index finger with the pointed part of the pick aiming directly at the strings.

The thumb is placed over the pick, covering 2/3 to 3/4 of the pick..

To place the right hand (with the pick) in playing position, rest the pick on the first string. The pick should be tilted upward slightly, rather than at a direct right angle to the string. The pick should stroke the string just over and to the back (towards the bridge) of the sound hole. Pick the first string down. The right-hand wrist should move slightly when the string is played, and the right arm should move slightly from the elbow. When playing strings other than the first, after stroking the string, the pick should rest on the next smallest string. This action is a type of **rest stroke,** which is commonly used in fingerstyle playing, and will generate a richer and fuller tone than picking with an outward motion will. Try playing each of the strings using this type of motion.

To get the feel of strumming with the pick, rest the pick on the fourth string and strum four strings down. Be sure to have a relaxed right hand. Move the wrist and arm slightly when doing the strumming. When picking a single string, or strumming, upward, the pick is tilted down slightly so the pick will glide across the strings, rather than "bite" or snag them.

Tuning

There are several methods which can be used to tune the guitar. One way to tune the guitar is to tune it to itself. You can tune the first string of the guitar to a piano, pitch pipe, tuning fork, or some other instrument, and then match the strings to each other. To do this, use the following steps:

▶ **1.** Tune the first open string to an E note. (Remember, open means that no left-hand fingers are pushing on the string.) You can use a piano, pitch pipe, tuning fork, or another instrument. If you use a tuning fork, use an "E" tuning fork. Hold the fork at the base and tap the fork on your knee, or another object, to get the fork to vibrate. Then, touch the base of the fork near the bottom of the bridge of the guitar. The pitch which will sound is the pitch the first string should have when the string is played open.

▶ **2.** After the first string is tuned, place a left-hand finger on the second string in the fifth fret. Play the first and second strings together. They should be the same pitch. If not, adjust the second string to match the first.

▶ **3.** Place a finger on the third string in the fourth fret. The third string should now sound the same as the second string open. If not, adjust the third string.

▶ **4.** Place a finger on the fourth string in the fifth fret. The fourth string, fifth fret should sound the same as the third string open.

▶ **5.** Place a finger on the fifth string, fifth fret. This should sound the same as the fourth string open.

▶ **6.** Place a finger on the sixth string, fifth fret. The sixth string, fifth fret should sound the same as the fifth string, open.

The diagram below shows where the fingers are placed to tune the guitar to itself.

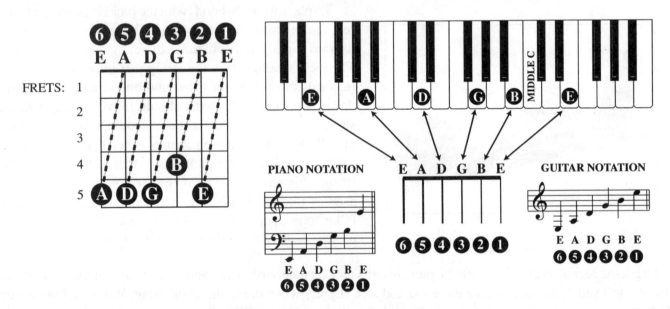

Another common method of tuning is the use of an **electronic tuner**. Tuners utilize lights (LEDs) or VU meters to indicate if a string is sharp or flat. Tuners have built in microphones or electric guitars can be plugged in directly. Follow the instructions provided with the tuner. If the tuner does not respond to playing a string, make sure you are playing the correct string and, if it is adjustable, the tuner is set for that particular string. Sometimes on the lower notes, the tuner won't function properly. If this happens, try playing the harmonic on the twelfth fret of the string. To do this, place a left-hand finger on the string over the twelfth fret-wire. Touch (do not push) the string very lightly. Pick the string. A note should be heard which will have a "chime" effect. This is a harmonic. It will ring longer if the left-hand finger is moved away from the string soon after it is picked. The electronic tuner will most likely respond to this note.

6

Reading the Music Diagrams

The music in this book will be written using chord diagrams, tablature and standard notation.

Chord diagrams will be used to illustrate chords and scales, With the chord diagrams, the vertical lines represent the strings on the guitar, with the first string being on the right. The horizontal lines represent frets, with the first fret being on the top. Dots, or numbers, on the lines show the placement of left-hand fingers. The numbers on, or next to the dots indicate which left-hand finger to use. A diamond may be used to indicate the placement of the root of the chord or scale. **Root** refers to a note which has the same letter name as the chord or scale.

A zero above a string indicates the string is to be played open (no left-hand fingers are pushing on the string). An "X" above a string indicates that string is not to be played, or that the string is to be muted by tilting one of the left-hand fingers and touching the string lightly.

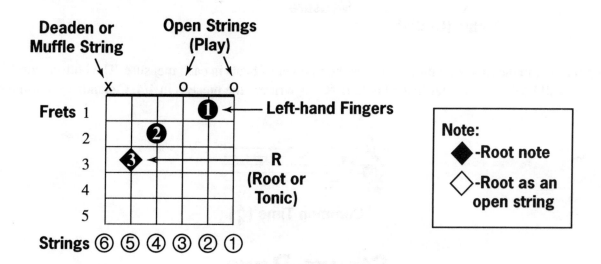

Left-Hand Fingers

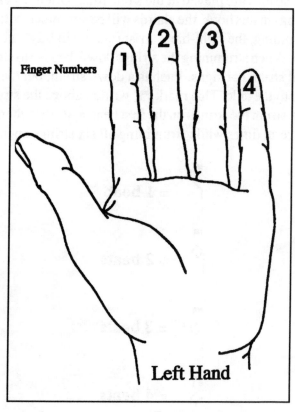

Music Fundamentals

The five lines and four spaces in music is called a **staff**. At the beginning of each line, a treble clef, or G clef, is written on the staff. The treble clef will be discussed later. The staff is divided into sections with **bar lines**. The sections between the bar lines are called **measures**. Inside each measure there are **beats**. Beats are the pulse of the music or measurements of time. The number of beats in each measure can be determined by looking at the **time signature.** The time signature is the fraction which appears at the beginning of the music.

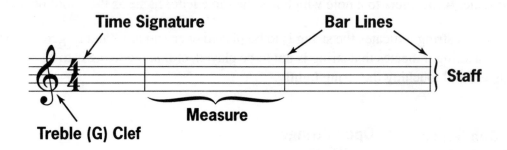

The top number in the time signature indicates the number of beats in each measure. The bottom number in the time signature will be discussed later in the book. If "C" is written, the piece is in 4/4. C stands for **common time**.

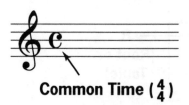

Common Time ($\frac{4}{4}$)

Strum Bars

A **chord** is when three or more strings are played at the same time. Often, when playing chords, the strings are strummed. For the exercises and songs in this book, the chords will be strummed with a pick. For the holding position of the pick, see page 7. When strumming, the right-hand wrist rotates slightly, and the arm moves from the elbow as the pick moves across the strings. When strumming the strings down, be sure to strum straight down. Do not strum outward. Written below are several strum bar signs. Each is a down strum, but the length of the strum varies. The time value of each strum is written to the side. This mark, ⊓, written above the strum bar, indicates a downstroke. If the strum gets more than one beat, strum the strings on the first beat, and allow them to ring for the additional beats. Practice playing each strum bar several times while strumming all six strings open. **Open** means that <u>no</u> left-hand fingers are pushing on the strings.

= 1 beat

= 2 beats

= 3 beats

= 4 beats

Practice the following rhythm exercise strumming all six strings open. Strumming the strings open may seem a bit strange at first, but the object is to play the correct rhythm and not be concerned with holding chords. Tap your foot on the beat (four times in each measure). The pick should be used to do the strum.

Open Chords

Shown below are numerous open chords. Open chords are chords that utilize strings that are not pressed down ("open strings") with the left-hand fingers. These chords are commonly used in country and folk tunes and are effective chords to use when accompanying a singer.

Major Chords

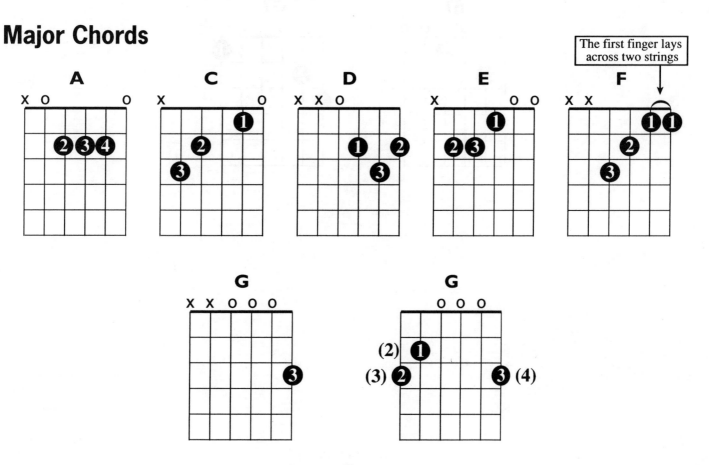

The first finger lays across two strings

Minor Chords

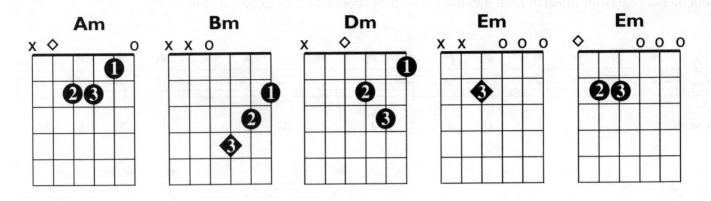

Seventh Chords

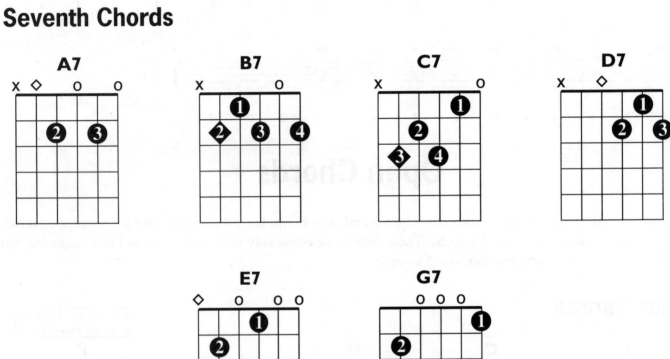

Practice the following exercises using down strums to gain control of the open chords. Each chord is assigned a quarter-note strum bar and should be strummed once for each beat. If strum bars are not present in each measure, play the strum pattern that is presented at the beginning of the progression.

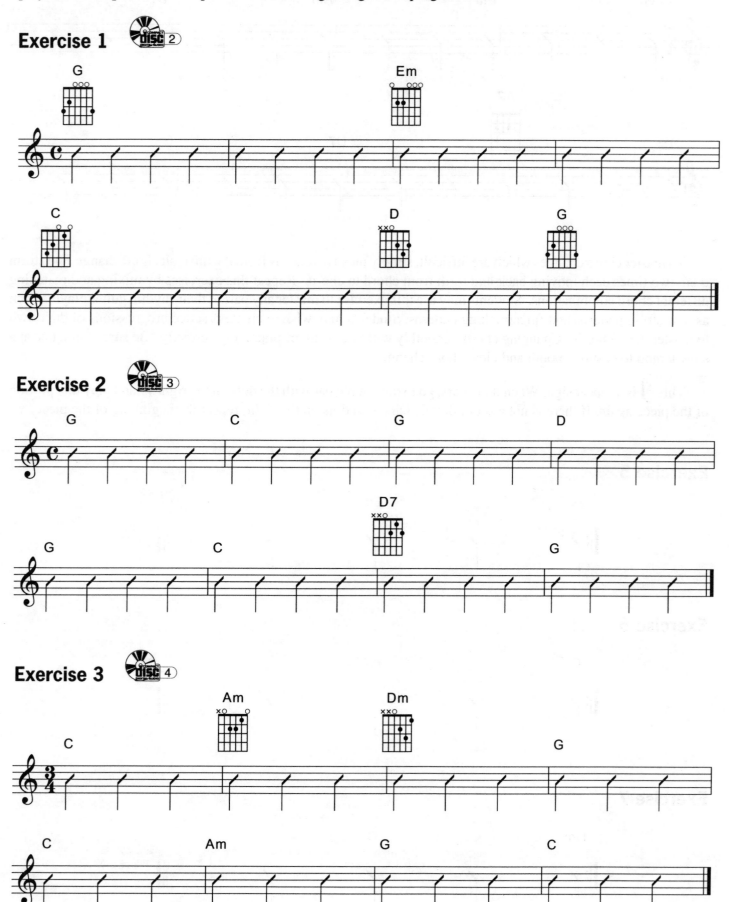

Exercise 4

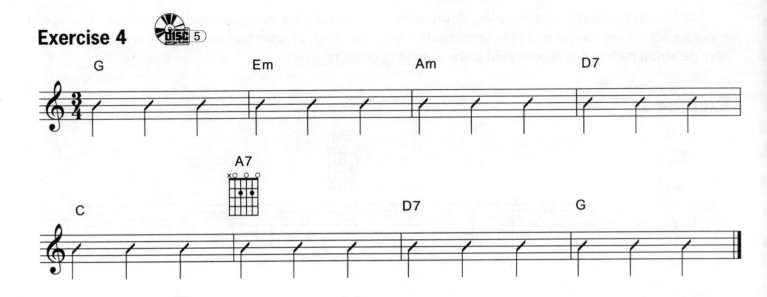

To master chord changes which are difficult, simply pick two chords from the difficult chord change and strum them two times each moving back and forth from chord to chord. Repeat this exercises by mixing and matching different chord combinations. Students may use this exercise to master any part of their rhythm guitar playing such as new strum patterns and fingerpicking patterns. Students may wish to create practice progressions of their own to master these chords. Changing chords smoothly will be a result of practicing correctly. Be sure to practice at a slow tempo to ensure smooth and clear chord changes.

This :‖ is a repeat sign. When it appears, go to the double bar with the dots on the right ‖: and play that portion of the piece again. If there is not a set of double bars with dots on the right, repeat the beginning of the piece.

Exercise 5

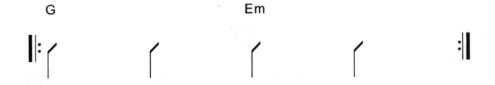

Exercise 6

Exercise 7

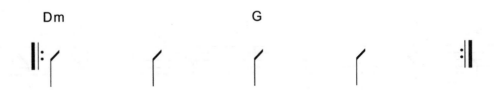

Strum Patterns

A **strum patterns** can be used to create interest to the accompaniment. A strum pattern can consist of a combination of down and up strums. A down-strum is indicated with this sign, ⊓, written above the strum bar. The up strum is indicated with this sign, V, written above the strum bar. Regardless of the chord being played, when doing an up-strum, only the first (highest sounding) three or four strings should be strummed. The pick should be used and angled downward slightly when doing the up-strum. When two strums are connected with a beam, they are called eighth note strums. When playing eighth-note strums, there are two notes played in one beat. The first strum bar is a downstroke and is played on the first half of the beat. The up-strum is played on the second half of the beat. The eighth-note strum is the strum equivalent to eighth notes in standard notation. Eighth notes will be presented later in this book. The downstroke is counted as the number of the beat on which it occurs, and the up strum is counted as "and," example:

one and

Very often, eighth-note strums are played using **swing rhythm.** In swing rhythm, rather than the beat being divided into two equal parts, the down-strum gets about two-thirds of the beat and the up-strum gets the remaining one-third of the beat.

If playing with swing rhythm is difficult at first, think of the melody to "Battle Hymn of the Republic." This melody is often sung with swing rhythm. If a tune is to be played using swing rhythm, often, is written at the top of the music. Practice the following exercise playing the down and up strums evenly. Then, repeat the exercise using swing rhythm.

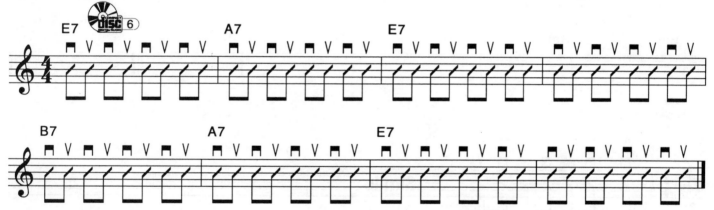

Written below are six strum patterns which are commonly used to play the blues. Each of the strum patterns take one measure of 4/4 to complete and can be used to play any blues song in 4/4. Once a pattern has been selected, play the same pattern in each measure of the piece. It is uncommon to combine patterns.

Practice holding any chord and play each pattern. Be careful to use the correct strum direction and correct rhythm. Tap your foot on each beat and count the rhythms aloud. The patterns are written in order of difficulty. Master one pattern before moving to the next.

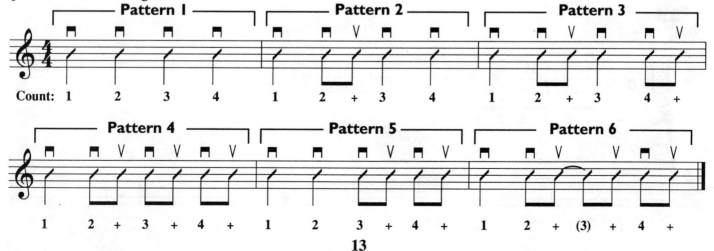

Notice pattern six contains a loop called a "tie." When two strum bars or two of the same notes are connected with a tie, play the first strum and allow it to ring through the time value of the second. Do not strum the second strum bar.

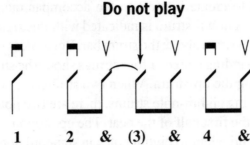

This :|| is a repeat sign. When it appears, go to the double bar with the dots on the right ||: and play that portion of the piece again. If there is not a set of double bars with dots on the right, repeat the beginning of the piece.

Practice the following three blues progressions. In each measure, use the strum pattern which is written is the first measure of the example.

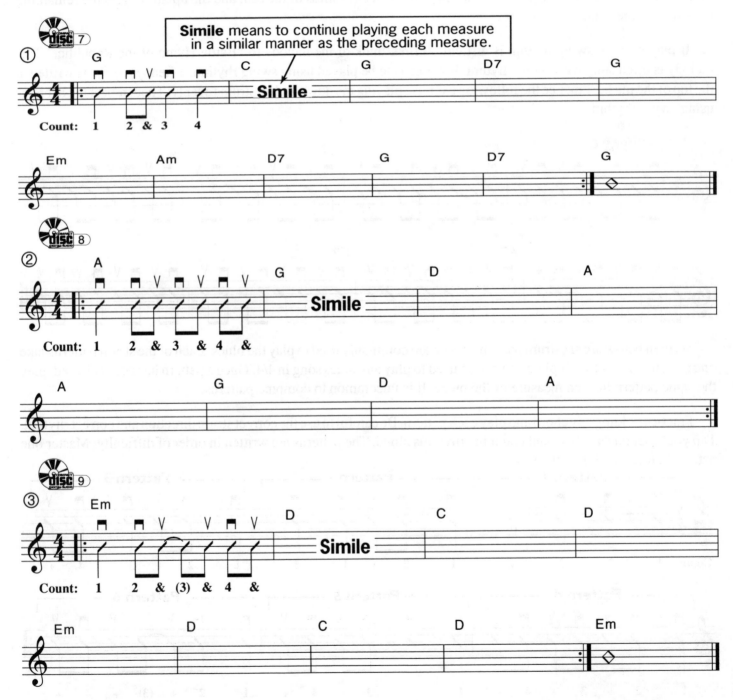

How to Read Standard Notation

Being able to read and write music in standard notation will be a great asset to any guitarist. Understanding standard notation makes it easier for guitarists to learn new music (especially if a recording is not available), write their ideas for other guitarists to play, and jot down ideas they may want to remember in the future.

The lines and spaces on which notes are written is called the **staff**. Guitar music is written in the **treble clef**. The treble clef sign will be at the beginning of the staff for music played on the guitar. The treble clef circles and identifies the second line from the botton as G. The treble clef is sometimes called the **G clef**.

The note names for the treble clef are shown on the staff below. The mnemonic (memory building) device commonly used to remember the notes on the lines of the treble clef is *Every Good Boy Does Fine*. The letters found in the spaces of the treble clef spell the word *FACE*.

The time values are the same for standard notation as they are for strumming notation. Time values for each note and rest are shown below for common time (C) signatures with a four as the bottom number (4/4, 3/4, 2/4 etc.)

𝆷	=	Whole Note	—	4 beats
𝅗𝅥	=	Half Note	—	2 beats
𝅗𝅥.	=	Dotted Half Note	—	3 beats (The dot adds to a note ½ its original value)
𝅘𝅥	=	Quarter Note	—	1 beat
𝅘𝅥.	=	Dotted Quarter Note	—	1 ½ beats
𝅘𝅥𝅮	=	Eighth Note	—	½ beat
𝅘𝅥𝅯	=	Sixteenth Note	—	¼ beat

Whole Rest 4 beats	Half Rest 2 beats	Dotted Half Rest 3 beats	Quarter Rest 1 beat	Dotted Quarter Rest 1 ½ beats	Eighth Rest ½ beat	Sixteenth Rest ¼ beat

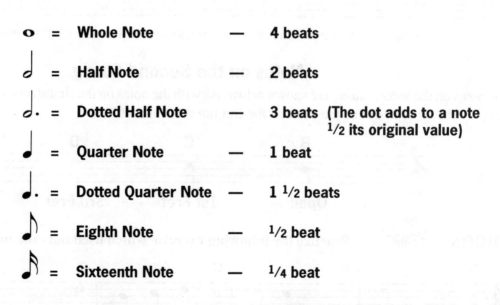

Standard Notation in First Position

While there are many notes on the guitar (one note for each string and fret), only standard notation in first position will be covered in this book. The term **first position** means that the first finger of the left-hand will be stationed or positioned at the first fret and will, therefore, play all the notes on each string located in that fret. This allows each of the left-hand fingers to play in the fret that corresponds with the finger number. The second finger is responsible for all of the notes in the second fret; the third finger plays the notes in the third fret and the fourth finger will play the notes found in the fourth fret. When playing in a higher position, the first finger determines the position, and the other fingers correspond to the frets just as they did in first position. For example, to play in the fifth position, the first finger of the left-hand is stationed at the fifth fret, the second finger in the sixth fret, the third finger in the seventh fret and the fourth finger in the eighth fret. Sometimes a Roman numeral is used in music and chord diagrams to indicate a position or fret number.

Notes on the First String

The notes on the first string are shown below. Remember, the first string is the smallest string on the guitar. The name of the note is written above the note, and the fret placement is written below the note. The number of the left-hand finger used to play the note should be the same as the fret number for that note. This is called **first position.**

Any Time 🎵 disc 10   Practice the following exercise which used only the notes on the first string.

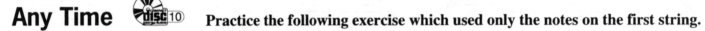

Notes on the Second String

The notes on the second string are shown below. As with the notes on the first string, the left-hand finger number used to play the note should be the same as the fret number for that note.

Choices 🎵 disc 11   Practice the following exercise which used only the notes on the second string.

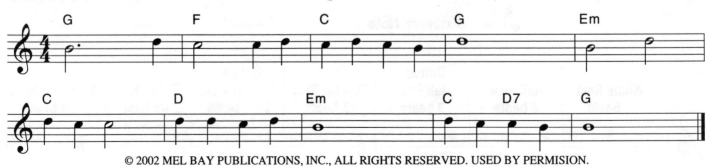

Notes on the Third String

The notes on the third string are shown below.

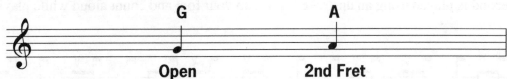

Open   **2nd Fret**

Think It Over

disc 12 Practice the following exercise which used only the notes on the third string.

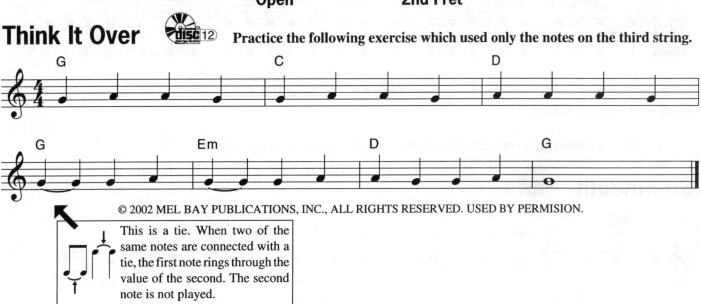

> This is a tie. When two of the same notes are connected with a tie, the first note rings through the value of the second. The second note is not played.

Under the Arch

disc 13 The next example combines the notes on the first three strings.

Eighth Notes

An eighth note looks like a quarter note with a flag attached to it (♪). If the bottom number in the time signature is a four $\frac{4}{4}$, the eighth note gets 1/2 beat. Two eighth notes gets one beat (♫).

Usually, two eighth notes are played in succession are connected with a bean ♫. When two eighth notes are played one after another, the first is coumted as the number of the beat in the measure on which it occurs, and the second eighth note is counted as "and."

Count: 1   and   2   and   3   and   4   and

If you are tapping your foot on the beat, the first eighth note is played when the foot is down and the second eighth note is played when the foot is up. When using a pick, generally, the first eighth note is played with a downstroke (⊓), and the second is played using an upstroke (∨). Tap your foot and count aloud while playing the following exercise.

An eighth note can be replaced by an eighth rest (⅞). If the eighth rest is written, rest (do not play or allow a string to ring) for 1/2 beat.

Practice the following exercise which contains eighth notes and eighth rests.

So Smooth

Sharps, Flats, and Naturals

Sharp, flat, and natural signs are shown below. They are called **accidentals**. When a sharp is written in front of a note, the note is played 1/2 step (one fret) higher. When playing a sharp note, be careful to use the same left-hand finger number as the number of the fret in which the note is played.

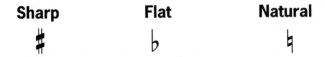

Play the following exercise using sharps.

Waiting for You

When a note has a flat sign in front of it, the note is played 1/2 step (one fret) lower. To flat an open string, go to the next lower string and find the fret where the lower string matches the pitch of the smaller open string. Then, flat the note by lowering it one fret. A chart showing the location of all the flatted open notes is shown below.

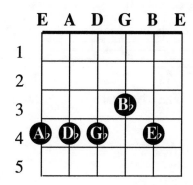

Practice the following exercises containing flats.

Loss for Words

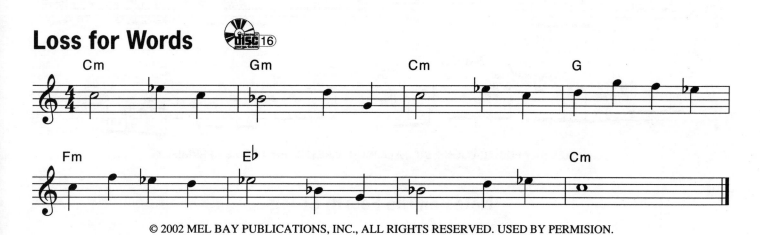

Freezing Point

* This E note is played on the fourth string second fret.

* This D note is played on the open fourth string.

* See page 20 for notes on the fourth string.

19

When a sharp, flat or natural sign is written in front of a note it not only affects that note, but it also affects all of the **same** notes which follow to the end of the measure. The bar line at the end of the measure cancels all previous accidentals. A natural sign cancels a previous sharp or flat. Practice the following examples containing accidentals.

Send Help

Notes on the Fourth String

The notes on the fourth string are shown below.

Fourth Gear

Practice the following exercise which used only the notes on the fourth string.

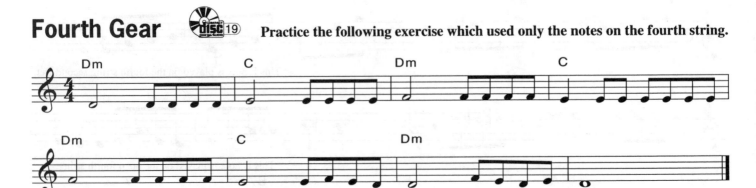

Notes on the Fifth String

The notes on the fifth string are shown below.

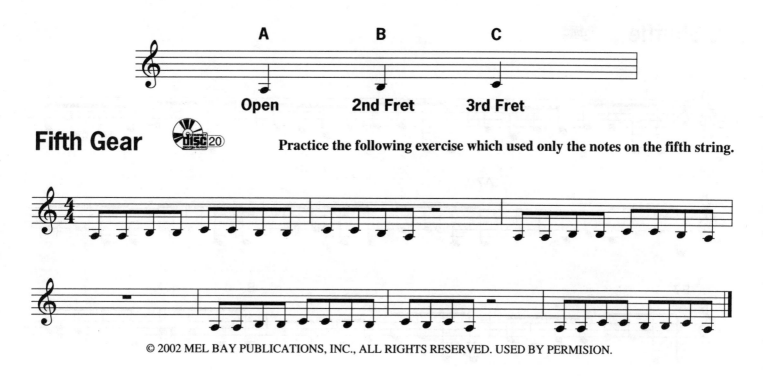

Fifth Gear

Practice the following exercise which used only the notes on the fifth string.

Notes on the Sixth String

The notes on the sixth string are shown below.

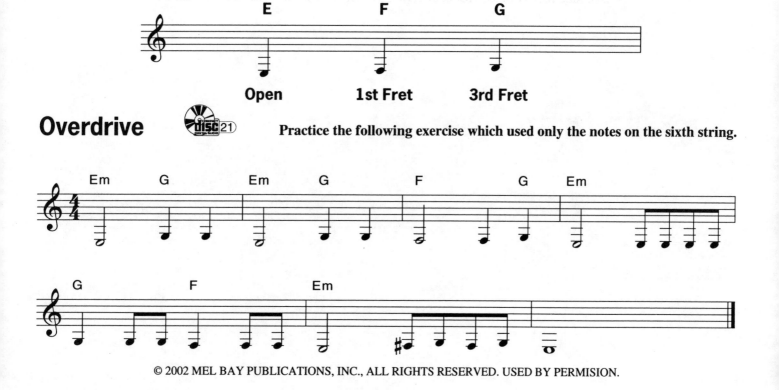

Overdrive

Practice the following exercise which used only the notes on the sixth string.

The next example uses the notes on strings four, five, and six and contains some accidentals.

E Shuffle

Power Chords

Power chords are **two-note chords** that are written with a 5 next to the chord name (A5). When playing power chords, be sure to pick both notes quickly so they sound simultaneously. Chord diagrams for the A, D, and E open power chords are shown below. In the blues, power chords are often used in place of seventh chords.

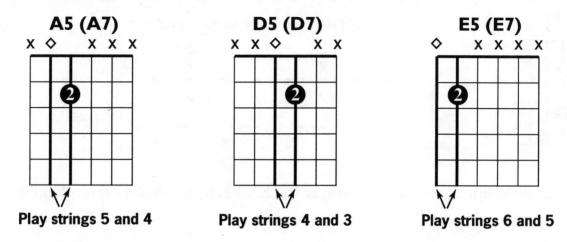

Play the following blues which uses open power chords. Even though eighth notes are used for this power chord strum pattern, use down-strokes only.

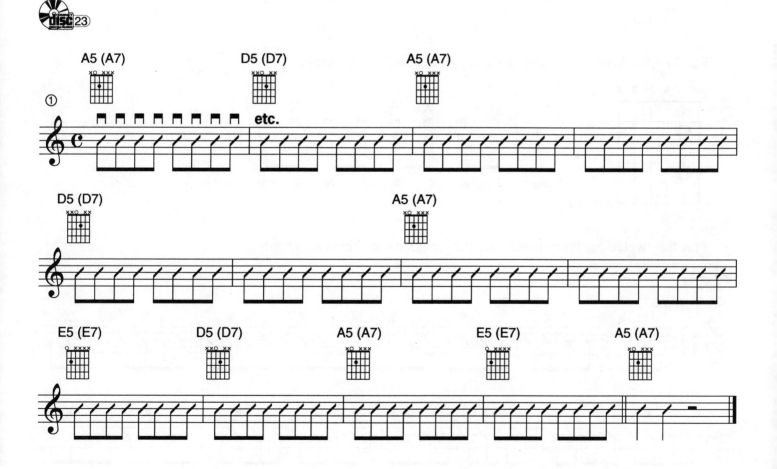

23

Power Chord Variation

A common variation on the power chord involves adding a finger on the third and seventh down-strokes (on the second and fourth beats) of the measure. For example, on the A5 chord, play strings 5 and 4 together four times. Use only down-strokes. On the third stroke, add the left-hand third finger where the "X" is drawn on the diagram below. On the fourth stroke, lift the third finger. Do this twice in each measure.

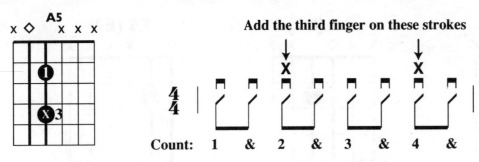

This technique could be used on the D5 chord by adding the third finger on the third string where the "X3" is drawn.

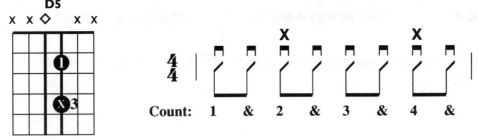

For the E5, add the third finger in the fourth fret on the fifth string.

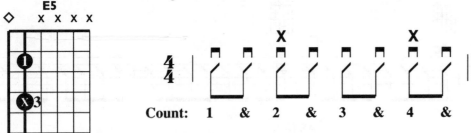

Play this twelve-bar blues which uses the variations on the power chord.

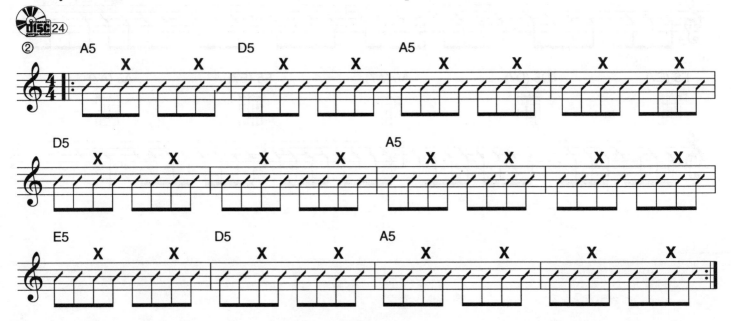

24

Tablature

Another way of writing guitar music is called tablature. The six horizontal lines represent the strings on a guitar. The top line is the first string.

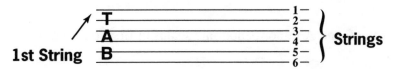

A number on a line indicates in which fret to place a left-hand finger. A stem connected to the number shows the note gets one beat.

Number indicates fret

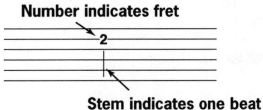

Stem indicates one beat

In the example below, the finger would be placed on the first string in the third fret.

1st String, 3rd Fret

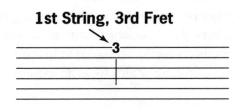

If two or more numbers are written on top of one another, play the strings at the same time.

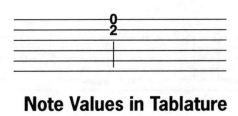

Note Values in Tablature

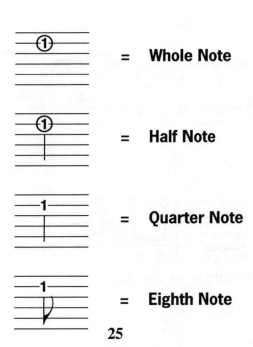

= **Whole Note**

= **Half Note**

= **Quarter Note**

= **Eighth Note**

Because the notes used in the solos for this section of the book are taken from scale patterns, and some patterns explore upper positions on the fretboard, the musical examples for this section of this book will be presented in tablature.

Minor Pentatonic and Blues Scales

Below are diagrams for the E and A minor pentatonic scales in first (open) position.

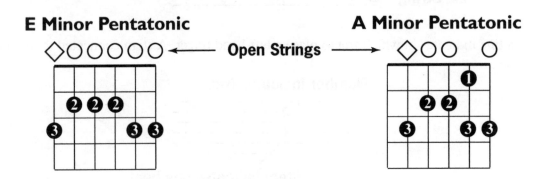

A pentatonic scale is a scale that contains five notes in an octave. Many guitarists use the minor pentatonic scale to create melodies and improvised solos over rock progressions. Use the E minor pentatonic scale when playing tunes in the key of E minor. Use the A minor pentatonic scale when playing solos in the key of A minor. The minor pentatonic scale used for the solo should have the same letter name as the key. This "key scale" is used to solo over the entire progression (even when the chords change). The solos below make use of the E and A minor pentatonic scale and demonstrate how a guitarist can use these scales to write melodies or play an improvised solo.

The Watchtower

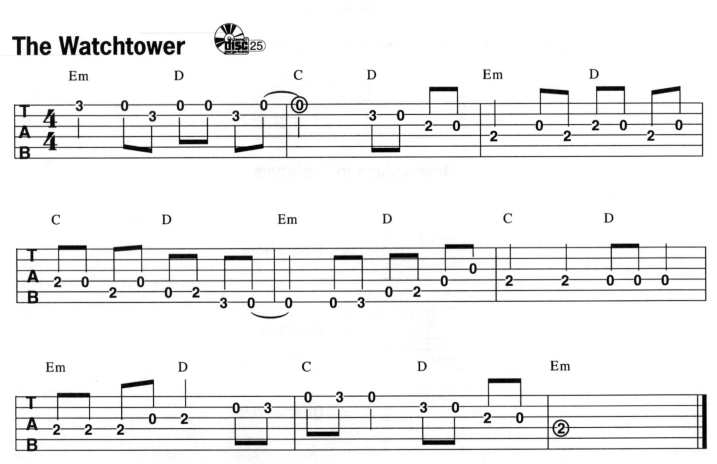

Flying High

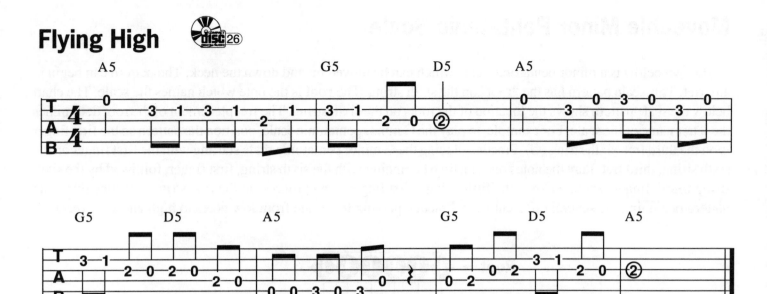

The blues scale has one more note per octave than the minor pentatonic scale. Some refer to this note as the **blue note** because it can have a harsh, dissonant sound. Diagrams for the open E and A blues scale are shown below. The circled numbers show the locations of the blue notes.

The blues scale can be used just as the minor pentatonic scale can be used to write blues melodies and play improvised blues solos.

Moveable Minor Pentatonic Scale

Drawn below is a minor pentatonic scale which can be moved up and down the neck. The pattern can begin in any fret. This scale pattern has the "root" on the sixth string. The **root** is the note which names the scale. The chart below the scale pattern shows the location of the roots on the sixth string. The fret placement of the root determines the letter name of the scale. For example, to play the G minor pentatonic scale, position the pattern so the first finger is on the third fret, sixth string (G). Practice playing the G minor pentatonic scale starting with the first finger on the sixth string, third fret. Play the notes one at a time beginning with the sixth string, first finger, followed by the sixth string fourth finger. Then, move to the fifth string - first finger - and progress to the first string. Practice this scale pattern beginning the several different frets. Practice playing this scale from low notes to high and vice versa.

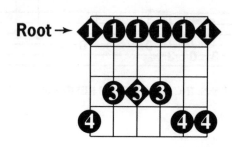

Fret	1	3	5	7	8	10	12
Root Name	F	G	A	B	C	D	E

To sharp the scale, move the pattern up one fret. For example, G♯ minor pentatonic scale begins in the fourth fret. To flat the scale, move it down one fret. For example, B♭ minor pentatonic begins in the sixth fret.

The scale pattern drawn below is the same minor pentatonic scale with the root on the sixth string. However, two circled numbers have been added. The addition of the circled **2** and **4** on strings five and three turns the minor pentatonic scale into a blues scale.

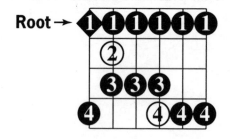

The following blues solo is in the key of A and uses the notes from the moveable minor pentatonic scale beginning on the sixth string, fifth fret (A). Remember, when a number is on top of another number, play the two strings at the same time.

Summer Blues, Summer Not

When improvising over the blues progression, any of the notes from the minor pentatonic scale can be used in the solo. The notes must come from the minor pentatonic scale which has the same letter name as the key. Even when the chords in the progression change, the notes used for the solo can come from the scale of the key. For example, when creating an improvised blues solo in the key of A, the notes used in the solo can come from the A minor pentatonic scale. Whether the chords are A7, D7, or E7, the A minor pentatonic scale can be used to play the solo because the entire progression is in the key of A.

Practice creating your own improvised solo to the progression at the top of this page and the blues in other keys by using the notes from the moveable minor pentatonic scale.

The pattern for the moveable minor pentatonic scale with the root on the fifth string is drawn below. The addition of the circled numbers will convert the minor pentatonic scale into the blues scale. Like the moveable scale pattern with the root of the sixth string, this pattern may be moved up and down the neck. Again, the letter name of the root will determine the letter name of the scale. The chart for the location of the roots on the fifth string is drawn below the scale pattern. Practice this scale pattern with, and without, the circled numbers.

Fret	2	3	5	7	8	10	12
Root Name	B	C	D	E	F	G	A

Licks

Constructing a rock or pop solo could be compared to baking a cake. The solo consists of several elements or ingredients which combine to make the final product. The type of ingredients used will determine the flavor of the cake, or in when soloing, the feel or mood of the solo. One of the ingredients which could be included to build a solo is called a **lick**. A lick is a series of notes which have a "catchy" sound. They may be repeated several times in a solo. They are so commonly used that they might be called "rock cliches."

Five rock licks are given below. Because rock solos which appear in magazines and on the internet are often written in tablature, the licks are shown in tablature and standard notation. Each lick can be played while the accompaniment (guitar or keyboard) is playing E7, Em, or/and E5 chord.

Practice each lick individually and then play the written solos which contain licks. After playing the written solos, practice improvising your own solos to an E7 or Em chord by combining these licks with the E minor pentatonic scale.

An *Sl.* above a slanted line going upward (⤴) before a note indicates to slide from two frets below the written note up to the note. An *Sl.* written above a slanted line going downward (⤵) indicates to slide from two frets above the written note down to the note. A circled number written next to a note indicates the string on which that note is to be played. For example, ③ would indicate to play the note on the third string. If you are in doubt of where to play the note, refer to the tablature.

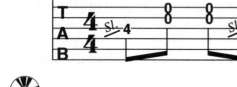

Lick #1

Note: Each lick has been recorded at a slow practice tempo and a faster performance tempo.

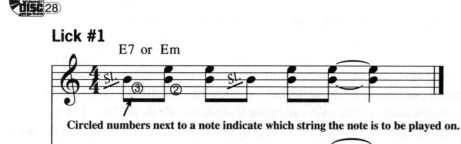

Circled numbers next to a note indicate which string the note is to be played on.

Lick #2

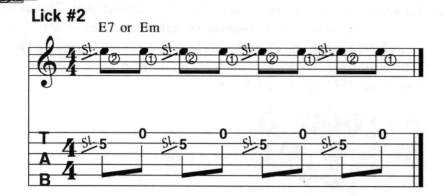

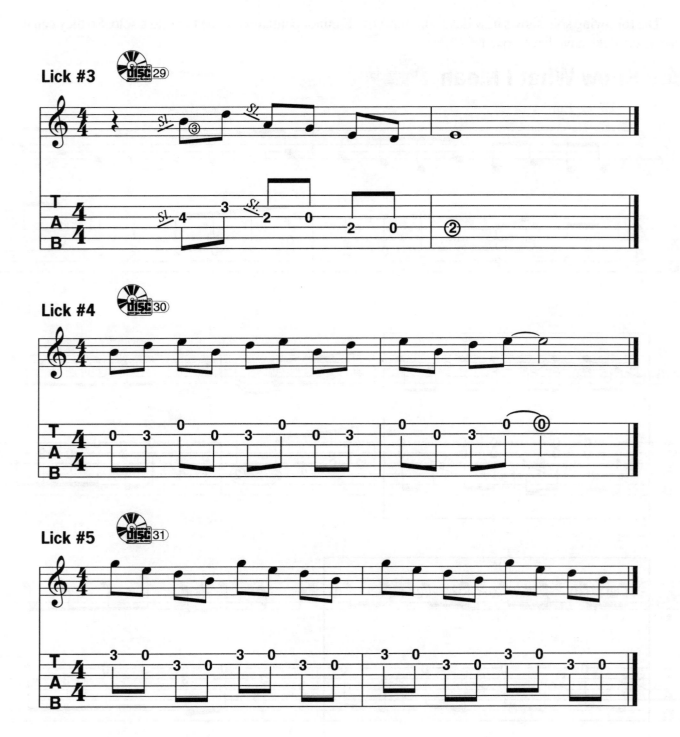

The following solo shows how licks combine with E minor pentatonic scale to build a solo. So they can be seen easily, the licks have been boxed.

You Know What I Mean

E7 or Em

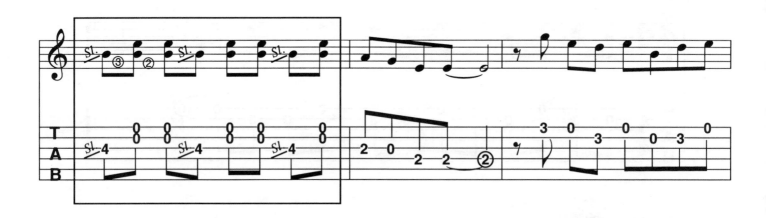

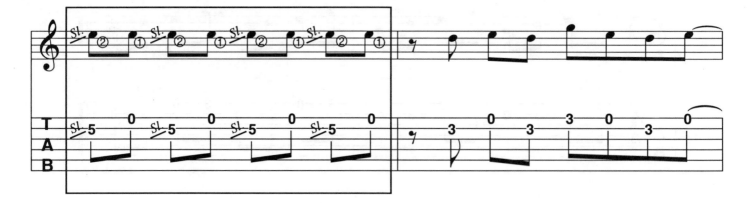

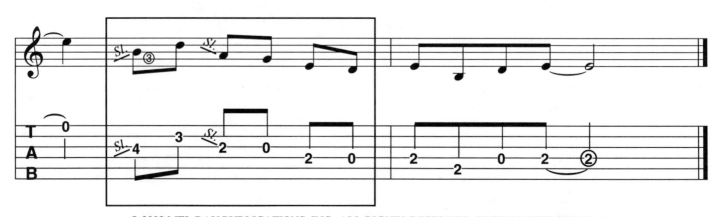

Moveable Power Chords

In order to play power chords other than A5, D5, and E5, open strings cannot be used. The diagram below shows a moveable power chord. It can be positioned anywhere on the guitar neck. When playing this chord, play only the strings which have fingers on them. The dot with the "R" pointing to it is the **root**. The letter name of this note will be the letter name of the power chord. The chart below the diagram shows the names of the notes (roots) on the sixth string and the frets numbers in which they are located. By using the chart below and moving the power chord pattern, it will be possible to play 12 power chords.

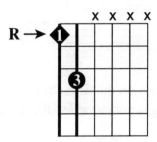

Sixth String Roots

Fret	0	1	3	5	7	8	10	12
Root Name	E	F	G	A	B	C	D	E

Moveable power chords may be played on any fret. For example, B5 would have the root in the 7th fret.

B5

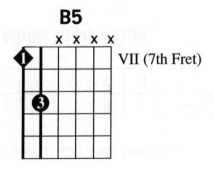

To sharp a power chord, move the pattern up one fret. To flat a power chord, move the pattern down one fret.

G♯5

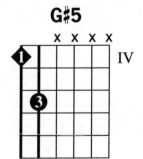

B♭5

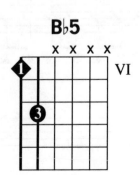

Practice the following exercise using power chords with the root in the sixth string. Play down eight times in a measure (two times to a beat.)

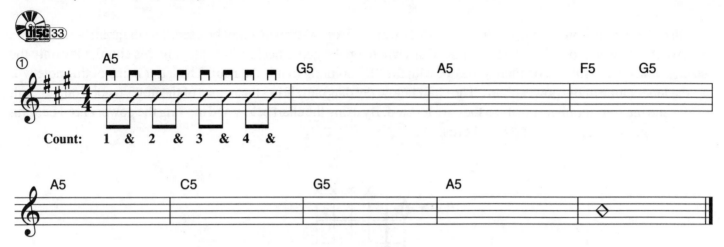

Power chords may also be played with the root on the fifth string. The diagram below shows how this is done. A C5 power chord with the root on the fifth string is positioned so the finger on the fifth string is in the third fret (C).

C5

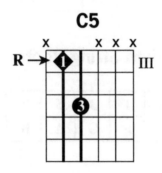

The chart below shows the locations of the note names (roots) on the fifth string.

Fifth String Roots

Fret	0	2	3	5	7	8	10	12
Root Name	A	B	C	D	E	F	G	A

Practice the following exercise using only power chords with the roots on the fifth string.

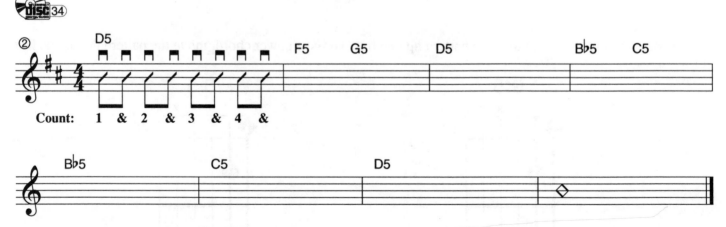

By combining power chords with their roots on the sixth and fifth strings, you can change chords and keep them positioned close to each other and avoid a lot of unnecessary position shifting. The R5 or R6 next to the chords, on the first line, indicate which string the root of the chord should be played on.

Practice the next exercise using combination of power chords with the roots on the sixth and fifth strings.

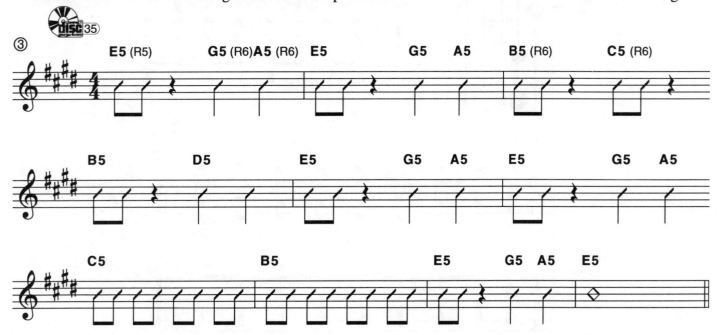

These "moveable" power chord patterns can also be modified by adding the sixth. This is done by playing the chord down four times. Be sure to play only the strings which have finfers on them. On the third stroke, add the left hand fourth finger where the "X" appears on the diagram. Lift the fourth finger off on the fourth stroke. Do this two times in each measure. Use only downstrokes. The diagram below shows how this technique is used on a power chord with the root on the sixth string.

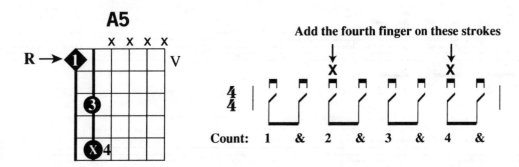

The following shows the notation and tablature for this technique for the A5 chord.

The next diagram shows how this technique would be used on a power chord with the root on the fifth string.

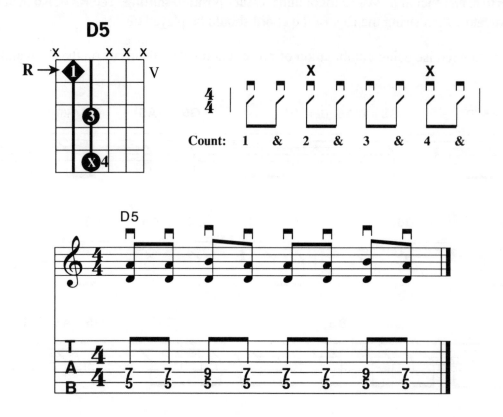

Practice the following exercise using moveable power chords with the addition of the sixth. Try to keep the chords close to one another by using power chords with the roots on the sixth and fifth strings.

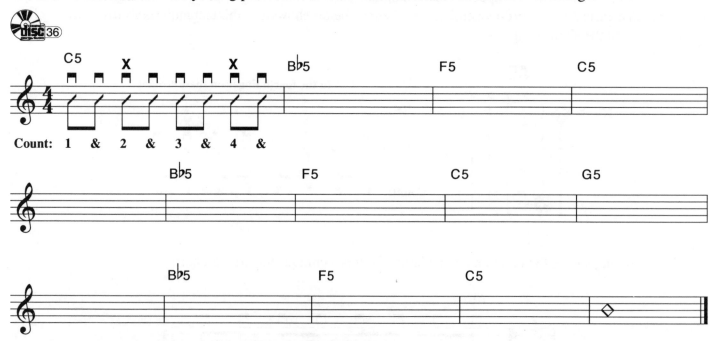

Play the following exercise using the variation on the moveable power chords.

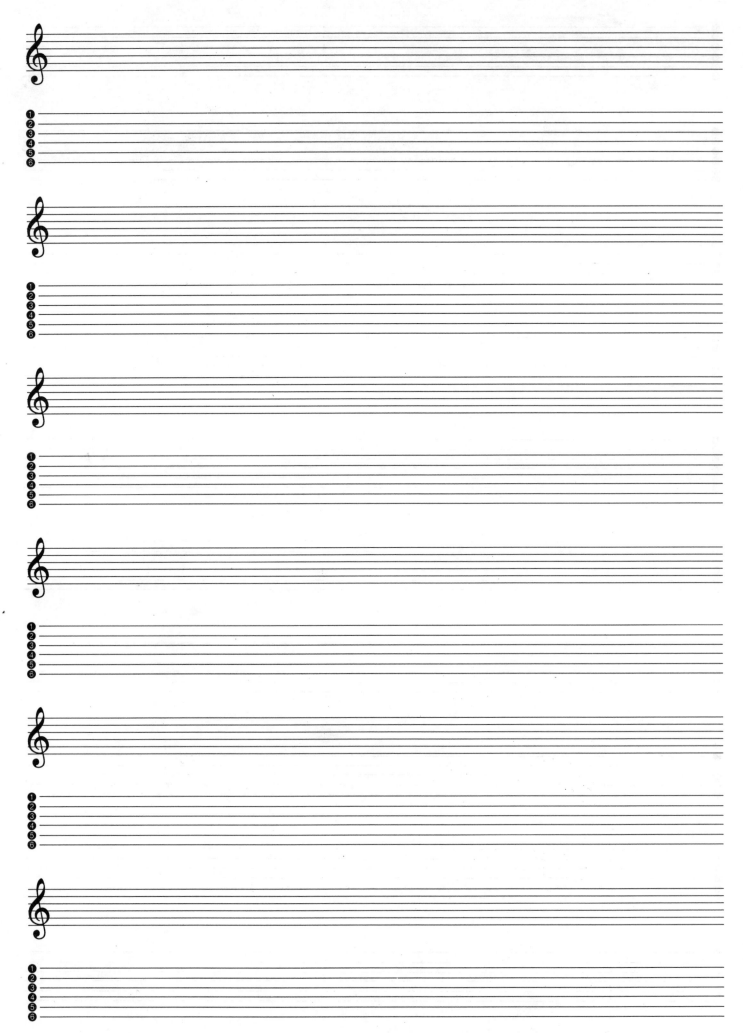